Carnevale

Jaye Tomas

Copyright © 2015 Jaye Tomas

All rights reserved

ISBN-13: 978-1515236351

Dedicated to the five brightest stars in my sky, and to any future ones I haven't met quite yet. The angels in my life have dirty, BEAUTIFUL faces. Nonna loves you to the moon and back.

"It takes courage to grow up and become who you really are."

~ *e e cummings*

"Don't be satisfied with stories, how things have gone with others. Unfold your own myth."

~ *Rumi, "The Essential Rumi"*

"You will hear thunder and remember me, And think: "she wanted storms.""

~ *Anna Akhmatova*

Copyright © Jaye Tomas 2015

No part of this bookmay be reproduced or performed without written consent from the author, if living, except for critical articles or reviews.

1st edition.

ISBN-13:978-1515236351

Cover designed by Sorell
Layout, proof reading and editing by David Ash
Type set in Times New Roman

Printed by CreateSpace

Jaye Tomas is Chimera Poetry

www.chimerapoetry.wordpress.com
www.facebook.com/jaye.tomas.7
www.facebook.com/chimerapoet
http://jayetomas.tumblr.com
Twitter : @JayeTomas1

To contact the author, email
jayetomas@gmail.com

To contact the artist, email
sorell.matei@yahoo.com

"The ink is always fighting to be heard…"

CONTENTS

Carnevale	10
Columbina	13
Doctor Death	15
Cinnamon Woman	16
School of Night	18
A Day of Bones	20
The Climb	22
Maybe It Was the Wine	23
Painting the Darkness	24
The Other Side of Midnight	26
Standing Aside	27
The Window	28
Le Théâtre Du Grotesque	29
Yellow Dawn	31
The Station	33
Disguised Poetry	34
Someday Soon	36
Sisterhood	37
The Dreaded	39
Alone She Dances	41
Under the Winter Sky	42
In the Graveyard	44
Strange Compass	46
Still Friends	48

Bella Donna	49
Static Days	51
The Bells	52
Pleurant	53
Borders	54
I Knew	56
The Tunnel	57
The Wonder Bus	59
Closets	60
Use Well the Day	61
Tatiana	62
I Soar Still	63
The Song of Stars	65
Ghost Writing	67
Naming Makes You Real	68
Spots On the Sun	70
Perceptions	71
Who Will Help Me Carry Him?	73
On a Train	75
I'm On A Train For Somewhere	76
A Deep Blue Lovesong	78
Building Dreams	79
Headaches	80
Telling Truths	81
The Toy Shop	83
Silver Coins	85

Seeing	86
Shadow Touch	88
Searching For A Lamp	89
The Best Days of My Life	90
Shifting Shadows	91
Glue	93
In the Midnight Garden	95
Medusan Dreams	96
The Color of Heartbreak is Yellow	97
Break the Sky	99
Burning Call	100
Awful Like Me	102
Machinery of Lost Memories	103
A Song of Separation	105
Dreaming Of Atlantis	107
She	110
Certain	111
I Never Should Have Followed	112
Mirror Dancing	114
City of Synapses	116
In My Very Bones	118
Cherry Wishes	120
Force of Nature	122
Poets	124
Grace, Bitter and Gone	125
In My Silence	128

Melissa	129
Keys	130
Keys 2	131
Keys 3 : The Door	132
Keys 4 : The Keymaker	133
Scar Tissue	134
This Is The End	135

Carnevale

Audaces fortuna iuvat.- Fortune favors the bold. ~ Virgil

Virtue has a veil, vice a mask. ~ Victor Hugo

Costumed in red and yellow they scamper through the streets
and knuckle the doors,
the hot sun pooling,
as if splashing,
pouring,
molten hot from a crucible,
around their feet.
The Carnevale is coming…

Porcelain, peacock blue, emerald green and gold mask the windows,
   the streets,
      the faces,
and the air is an elixir
and the very stones smell of chocolate,
of figs,
of sour spilled wine and orange peel.
Stained by magic old and new,
by sex and mystery and rainstorms.

Demons and Courtesans eye each other familiarly
while the golden tower is carried through the square
and a humming cry spirals up from the crowd,
its energy bending and glowing as if the moon were melting.
"Beads my darling?"
the vendors sing.
"Beads?"
They tempt you with their tree of swaying strands,
the gold, the silver, the scarlet,
all the colors of alchemy.

Jugglers and fortune tellers and disappearing doves,
prayers of the faithful
and faithless alike in a cacophony of rich wanting,
of craving,
of coveting.
Masks make fortune and her other lesser-known sisters much bolder,
and nothing more than breathing in the river of scent can bring a flush to your face.
And the feeling rises in you until you are sure its vibration can be heard by others,
like the buzz of human cicadas,
as if you are Orpheus' lyre
and will lead them out...
or back.
Look up and gasp at the flight of the angel
and then clasp each others' eyes as if to confirm it was seen
and let the details dance past you,
red eyes,
red wine,
parasols of black web lace,
painted smiles.
The Carnevale is here.

Senses swim and clutch for more befuddling
as the sweetest of vices call,
echoing like deep-night fox song.
Around every corner a tableau plays out,
some comedy,
some art,
in real or restrung time.
Watch...

He stared,
she held a finger to her lips,
"Shhhhh."

*He wondered where she found a mask with wings
and then she flew away.*

Count them all,
like the seconds after a lightning flash,
sweets and eggs and candles in windows,
or guttering on gravestones grown suddenly fresh,
and the music plays all around you but no musician is present,
and that does not surprise anyone.
Not here,
in this uncreated night,
this wild revelry,
this Carnevale.

Columbina

Columbine,
Columbina,
dance with me through the streets of beaded windows
and wine washed cobbles.
Tie a string of sorrowful songs into your hair and let them
flutter as the wind
washes us with spice and gold spinnings,
catching on the pearls of your mask
and shining like dragonfly wings.
Columbine,
Columbina,
a night of magic and a day of wonder
with jugglers of butter-yellow suns
and a waltz never played before
because, at its merest tone,
the weeping would overrun the rivers.
But still we dance,
my Columbine...
my Columbina and I.
Little dove in the starlit alley with the incense wrapping you
like a burnt sugar cocoon.
This carnival,
this pageantry,
a stage for you to shine like the moon,
like the secret chamber of a nautilus shell.
These sinister diamonds
all in velvet laid out like a carpet
of finest Persian to tempt your touch,
to tease your flashing feet,
and we pirouette in the rosy dawn.
We unravel the clouds and weave them into portents to drop
like crystal balls in the gypsies' tent.
I will play for you a mandolin of sighing zephyrs,
dark winds and skies that do not flicker,

do not lighten
but only deepen,
infused in ancient and delicious sin.
Columbine,
Columbina,
My Columbina....

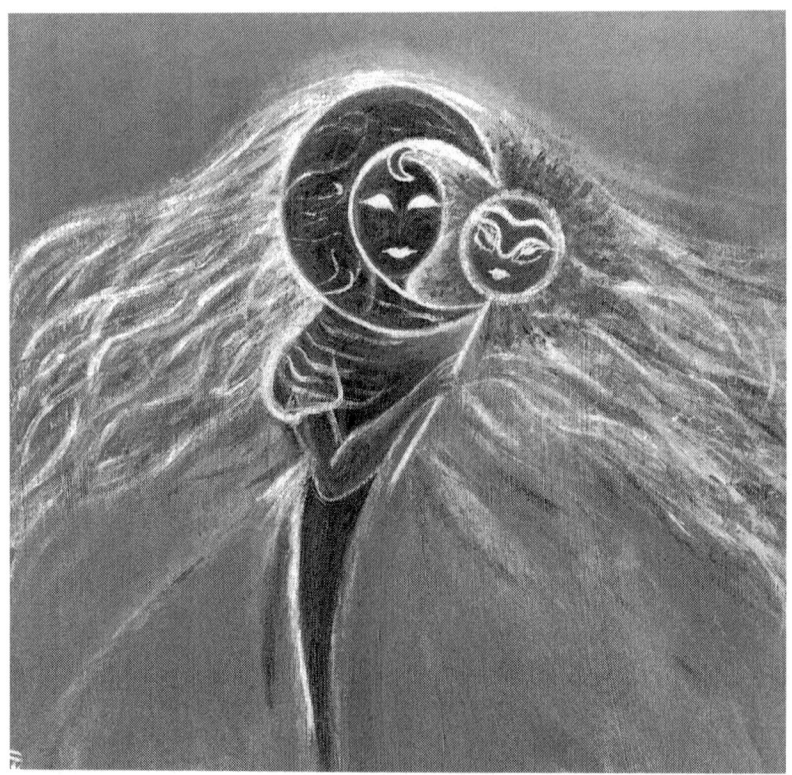

Doctor Death

Nose of beak
of bone
and eyes that burn like coals,
like smoke before the fire bursts free.
He walks through the crowd unrecognized,
unhailed,
but felt....
like a frisson of lightning along the back of the neck.
A place clearing before him as if by unseen rope
pulling the crowd back and tucking in their corners.
He scents his prey like a bear at a river bank
and this parade of revelers cannot hide the doe from him.
Time beats loud and louder in his temple and the clocks
mock him for his hurry,
but the gift he brings her will not wait...
One touch is all the performance this doctor will require
to bring the lily to her face
and stop the fluttering butterfly heart.
As he smiles and walks swiftly, surely away
the scent of cypress and poppies in his wake.
Another round of calls to make
and the light behind his grim and gaunt eyes burns brighter....

Cinnamon Woman

Cinnamon woman,
gliding in on a trail of cloves,
its spiced oil smoothed into the teak and topaz perfection of
her face,
and the light fractures starlike as it dances away from her
mere wisp of a mask,
the barest ribbon and lace molded against her eyes as if held
by spells and spiderwebs.
Her crescent moon lips curve as you inhale,
dragging the drugging tastes of clove and cinnamon,
filling your mouth and mind with it,
wrapping it like a lover's veil,
like an ancient goddess's benediction,
while the desire enfolds and presses your neck in a gallows
embrace
and digs its painted nails into your ribcage...
And the night deepens around your eyelids bringing welcome
waters to wash your memories away
as the air slows around you,
time bending and flexing,
ringing like a crystal goblet
and a burning violin pounds in your neck
surges through your fingertips and
trails sparks up your spine.
And you can almost hear the sizzle as the stars burn out
one by one
behind the curved and inviolate dome
of your eyes.
There is no mask that can shield you from this knowing,
this meeting,
this joining of blood to blood.
And in the silence between heartbeats
there is acquiescence,
there is power

and there is no shame,
for in that ultimate, blazing moment
the gazelle can deny the lion nothing.

School of Night

You promise to reveal the unknowable,
for all mysteries unravel before you;
the apple offers up to you
all its knowledge of good and evil,
or so you say
"Just walk with me
and believe...."
Against my better judgement,
the daylight,
normal
judgement,
I nod
and no sooner does my chin dip
than I feel a scream building in my chest
and my life passes,
not before my eyes,
but away from them...
What master are you
and what can be taught in this school of night,
this well of darkness that you toss me into?
Holding me down in thrashing terror
after cajoling me into this precipice walk
this twilight stroll
through the spaces in between
dark and light,
night and day,
the wanted
and the unwelcome,
the stars spawning overhead and the ground seething
beneath,
where I am held as surely as if compelled
in the crossroads,
observing the boundary,
readying for the subject taught only once.

There is no median,
only pass or fail,
life or death,
in the school of night.
And my soul screams for amnesia
as the lessons begin....

A Day of Bones

A day of bones
a day of bones
and breaking sticks and stones...
A day of lying undetected
under hot sand and bleaching.
A day of being still
and being hungry and hunted
and sorry...
for in the sand you feel the secondhand warmth,
but can't ever see it golding across your face;
can't grasp the light that your eyes crave like a drug,
the trembling fall of brightness, tumbling like motes through
the sifted air,
is lost in the rasp
and in the motion denied...
Hold
and the bones stay still
in sin and in secret.
Hold,
and the rods and cones run their machinery overtime
to keep the color locked tight within,
and the bones lock
to keep the trembling at bay.
Burrowing in all soft and fat,
you hold,
hold,
for the sand dollaring,
the hardening of your inner and outer self.
While the curtain calls for retribution not redemption in your
rerunning dreams.
For in the simplest and most dispassionate of truths
there is no white charger,
the flying monkeys are out of control,

your knights are trembling with you in other, separate burrows,
and the day plods by....
Your cocoon gently strangling as you helplessly watch the sand settle in more tightly around you
and your bones accept this with resignation
and any brief and random thought of emerging smothers itself in self-preservation.
A day of bones,
a day of bones,
a day of breaking,
of sticks and stones.

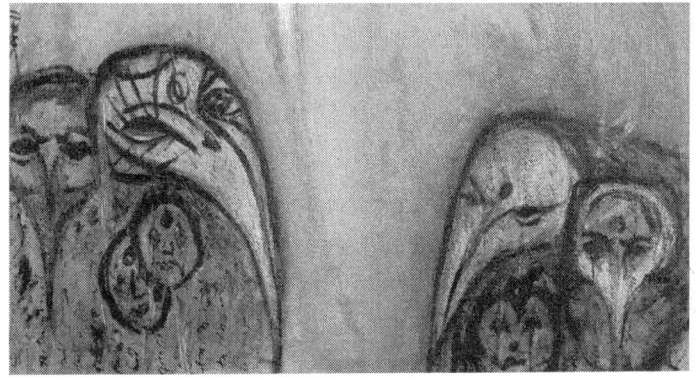

The Climb

It's a hard hike up into the misted mountains
and they say
that, looking back down,
if you gaze carefully
you can see,
blending in among the rocks and obstinately gripping plants,
those who came before you,
those who fell before you,
looking up
in warning?
in jealousy?
while the falcon and the goat make a mockery of your painful ascent.
You feel the wind blowing fresher, fiercer here,
as if touching the earth causes it to act softer,
more restrained...
All the while, the summit whispers your name
and the clouds bounce it to you.

Why do you climb? they ask,
Why do you stay low? you wonder,
for the closer to the sky you get,
the less you weigh,
until your last burden slips away,
hitching a ride on one of those fiercer winds,
like a kite snapping its tether,
kicking free;
and you feel the sun shining through you in your lightness,
glowing like oiled paper.
As you reach the hard-won pinnacle, you stand tall,
dizzy in the thinning flame-bright air,
then look up into the corridor of clouds
and know that you have not reached the end of your climb.

Maybe It Was the Wine

Maybe it was the wine,
the way it went to my face and bloomed there
like a dragon's kiss;
maybe it was the way your eyes crinkled as you looked at me,
like I was important to you.
Maybe it was the wine,
or maybe it was the music,
the songs we sang on the radio,
that day we drove our sinking heels across the dunes,
searching for the perfect sand dollar
and you counted the freckles on my nose and the seagulls in the sky
and it all added up to love.
Maybe it was the night,
maybe it was the terrible night
when I cried
and cried,
while you stared at me with the flat and lifeless eyes of a gila monster
right before you went out the door
in a trail of expensive cologne and whisky
and my heart shook until the sun came up,
shook and shook,
then it finally ran down
and I never wound it again,
just left it in its box, cradled in tissue paper and some broken bits of shell;
and then I opened a bottle and poured
and kept pouring until my mind finally stilled
and all I could taste were old tears;
or maybe it was the wine.

Painting the Darkness

"I am a forest, and a night of dark trees: but he who is not afraid of my darkness, will find banks full of roses under my cypresses." ~ Friedrich Nietzsche, *Thus Spoke Zarathustra*

A labor of love
of inspiration and dedication.
I worked carefully and thoroughly with exquisite care
and attention to every detail,
Sometimes with grand strokes,
with sweeping waves of paint
and then other moments with tiny barely-there dustings,
mere shadows on the canvas.
My brushes grew as worn and wracked as my body
until finally,
finally
it was time to unveil (birth) my creation.
They looked and looked
and looked again and said,
"It's all black..."
I said, "It's the darkness.
Darkness covering like a silken gown,
like the surrounding of a seed before it heeds the summons to reach,
like the birthplace of diamonds,
like the rivers from your heart that flow silently.
Dark like ink,
like the moon's hidden face,
like midnight.
I have poured the universe out before you,
here for you to marvel at,
to seek its wonders in the oil of its shadowed face,
in the mystery lying as close to you as your shuttered eyelid

and pressing in around every window dropped and fastened
against the terrors of the night.
Darkness with all its beginnings and endings,
rituals and murmurs,
spilling its secrets out from this wall."
And they looked again
and puzzled over what they perceived as mere lack of light
or absence of color
and my lack of understanding;
and then they laughed
and dismissed me.
And then I showed them real darkness.
The merciless darkness that borders,
that rings a raging pyre.
Later,
much later,
I cleaned up.
And began to paint again.

The Other Side of Midnight

Meet me on the other side of midnight,
the place of song endings.
Hold me up so I can touch the sky, the stars, the moon...
Shall we dance among the wishing wells,
dropping so many copper pennies in each one
that the wishes overflow and escape?

Meet me on the other side of midnight,
at the corner of Camelot and Oz,
and bring some sunflowers to fill the empty vases along the alleyways,
to light the walls as we write the story of our names on them,
with the shadows capering like plumage around our faces,
as we sign them with melting wax and kisses.

Meet me on the other side of midnight
to board the Atlantean trolley leaving soon.
The seafoam already gathers itself in great and pluming fountains
as a welcoming sign,
a signal
as we round the bend, crossing to the other sides,
where midnight is just approaching,
like fog on little cat feet
and we will meet
and we will meet
and we will meet once again.

Standing Aside

You see me walking away and remark in a cutting voice -
pitched to be heard -
how standoffish I am:
"She doesn't have much spark does she...?"
Spark?
Look past the seedy exterior needing new paint
and some rigorous landscaping.
Look inside.....
I'm the spark that sets a forest ablaze.
I'm a volcano goddess exploding without warning,
without mercy.
I'm lightning and winds that shriek down from mountains
that our ancestors prayed to and tried to placate.
I don't waste my words on you
because, once that gate is lowered,
the torrent pours unchecked and your imprint may not be
found for a millennium...
So I stand aside.
It's a cold place,
a solitary place,
so familiar that my feet have worn grooves.
I let the rain fall on my face and my feelings
and wonder that my cheeks don't steam.
The world is a wonderful place for those who don't walk with
their shadows,
but trying to find your place in the sun
can be difficult for one who melts.

The Window

I don't look out the window any more.
The frost has crept across the glass and across my heart as well.
The sunlight invites from the other side of the pane,
plays sweetly over the rooftops;
but my eyes turn inward
to the hardening icebound center of me,
the beats booming like breaking polar caps
and I don't look for saving
or warmth anymore.
It's easier this way.
My guardian angel finally packed up and went south,
because the frostbite from my shoulder clipped her wings
and these words I pen
are crystallizing on the page,
crisping like autumn leaves captured in an icy puddle;
and I hope the color holds,
because there is no reflection from me to lend them depth.
I don't look out the window any more,
with my fingers leaving hot penny circles.
I don't want to look.
I don't want to know.
I just want to settle back
and wait for the final, frigid moment
when both time and my burnt finger feelings freeze.
And perhaps later I can start to listen for the clock,
the calendar,
the seasons,
the single-minded sweeping of the moon,
to tell me when it's safe to exhale again.
To draw in a warm breath bravely,
to step over to the window and once more
look out.

Le Théâtre Du Grotesque

With eyes safely lidded and every neck bent,
a collective sigh drizzles along the crowds edge as you,
the Queen of Le Théâtre Du Grotesque,
arrive. Surging in on an upswell of terrorsweat and adoration,
your followers in a cluster of sycophantic clucking
scurry behind.
Flaunt, swirl your cloak and smooth your gloves
to allow those grandiose gesticulations.
You use your lorgnette in the wide arm blessings like a
conductor and his baton,
tied with ribbon and bits of mirror,
a crazy house reflection of the gilt and glimmer and the
spider webs decked in their finest silk.
The murmur rises as you part the red velvet curtains hanging
dustily in all their malicious opulence
and regally take your place in the box,
a window shop for the eyes, slyly tracking movements,
storing greedy grasping details with a flick of a paintbrushed
eyebrow.
An incense of burning books and footlights
heating the cedar planks
drift and hang like Spanish moss among the beams and cords,
a tangle of electric flowers.
One may imagine a misshapen figure skimming down, hand
over gnarled hand,
a half-masked face sneering;
but imagining is not taken for granted here,
not dismissed with bedtime soothings,
for the Théâtre has its own programs
and a thousand soft bodies like opened oysters
for its plundering.
Let the lights dim.....
and the music swell from Below,
as the cast march forward in their extravagant,

enhanced
costuming with lace and leather and wings and horns
and stitched-on smiles,
metal meeting flesh in violent metamorphosis,
a blend of tender skin and beaten copper scales to flash and
dazzle the crowd,
who never notice
the faintest whiff of laboratory
underlying the pungent pomade of roses and cloves
slicked on before the disciples heeded the curtain calling.
And you lean forward in the box above
betraying your horrific appreciation
as you count the rising gasps as sweet as coins.
A satisfied curve of your flagrant lip
as pity stuffed clumsily with sawdust arrives on stage as
(garnish) mere decoration;
for this grotesque troupe had no one left
qualified to play that role.....

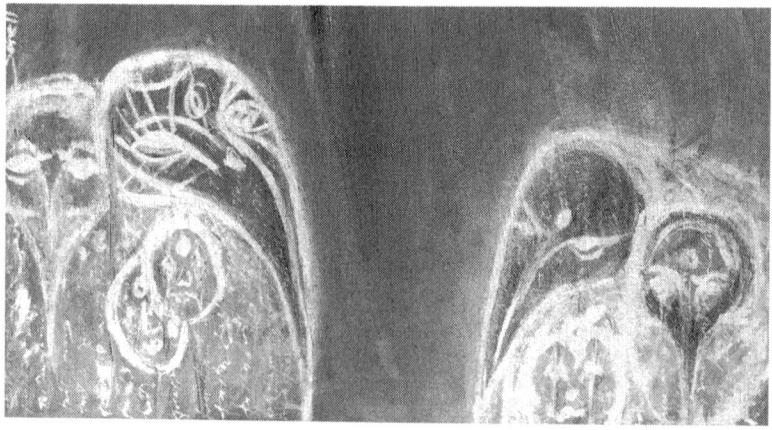

Yellow Dawn

"Red sky at night; shepherds' delight, red sky in the morning; shepherds' warning."

Red skies are recognized,
sung and painted and pointed at with pleasure.
They are an earthly known,
they are...
expected.
But what does a yellow dawn announce?
Is it a warm lemon sky,
one which warms the hands and ripens winter cheeks?
Or a sulphurous expanse filled with portentous grey
cloudriders?

It was so easily ignored,
this pale light splashed like urine across the empty sidewalks,
until it turned and bit the feeding apathetic hand,
shifted without warning into
the harbinger of wild destruction,
funnelling across the earth like a screaming wilful
locomotive.

Another yellow dawn, an alien sunrise.
Here I stand in the midst of mist
gazing at the light
and shadow,
desperately trying to sort,
to place the citron air into an understandable,
a sane
classification;
but its unearthly tones swirl around me
teasingly,
maliciously,
and while I twist and turn,

trying to avoid the chill sending its questing filaments down
my neck and spine,
my ears are slowly opening to the chthonian voices
whispering in unnatural bliss,
seeking to draw me,
to absorb me
into the delicate travesty
of this yellow dawn.

The Station

The station is lined with strangers,
like sparrows on a wire,
all clutching their dreams in carefully-bagged,
zip-locked,
freeze-dried,
safety-netted
compartments,
checking their tickets over and over again
in case the destination had decided to change;
as the birds perform their winged waltzes overhead
and the leviathan ships rise and fall,
closer,
riding the tides of the wind,
the zephyr,
while the birds drop seeds for her to bless.

Disguised Poetry

I keep them up my sleeves,
hidden,
secret,
like silk scarves,
like flashing coins,
like onion-skinned old letters.
I disguise them,
blend them into the fabric of my living day,
like raven feathers in the dark;
and sometimes,
sometimes I grow bold
and hand you one,
a treasure,
a curiosity,
and I shake a little
inside,
where the trembling only shows itself in the hitching of my
pulse,
hoping you will see it shine,
see it tumble,
glittering,
and you will love its fire
and its color and look at me with gladness,
with understanding,
and say, "Yes,
yes I see it,"
and smile....
But, like a child hating its playpen,
you smash it,
crush it beneath heavy words like duty
and obligation
that march in straight lines down narrow paths.
Can't you join me,
just for a moment?

Can't you try and see the poems in the spider webs?
I could read them to you.
Will you listen?
Or will you turn and scan the sky restlessly,
relentlessly
searching for the cloud you know must be there
to mar the blue perfection,
sighing when you find one;
your proof of the fractured,
the flawed,
a stain,
and yet a cloud so perfect,
such a compliment to the wide sky,
that painters weep to view it and with joyful thumbs,
smudge ivory on to their canvas?
And I quietly,
with scarcely shaking hands,
thread the scarves back into my sleeves,
still the light with hushed promises,
let it fade back into Pandora's cabinet
and wait ...
until my pulse smooths
and another window cracks slightly open.
Maybe this next time
we can read the poems together
and celebrate the spider's insight,
eyes brimming over with their brilliance.
Maybe this next time
the magic will be enough
to illumine the sideways staircases
tucked along the narrow paths
and bright enough to penetrate the disguise.

Someday Soon

Someday soon,
I promise myself,
I will call you on the phone and have something to say.
I will make you laugh,
make you feel stable
and loved and appreciated.
I will say,
"See you later,"
and really mean it...
Someday soon,
I shall collect some light remarks,
some amusing stories,
and press your hand.
Someday soon, I will spend the time
without impatience,
without grudging,
without hating it behind my eyes
and hoping you can't see,
without playing a brittle role.
Someday soon, I will not allow you to invent a heavy
schedule for me,
will not have to smother irritation.
Someday,
someday soon,
I thought I would.
I planned to...
And then you died.

Sisterhood

Sisters....hmmm?
Well, that patronizing downward chin-waggle, scrape-me-off-the-bottom-of-your-manolos look you are glasscutting
across the room at me
doesn't really speak much of,
doesn't really define
sisterhood.
Why do we topple our sisters?
Why does a woman look at another woman
in That Way?
You know the one....
the one only another woman recognizes as a challenge,
a gauntlet thrown down;
but instead of an armored glove,
a freakishly plucked eyebrow
tilted in your obviously inferior direction,
often accompanied by a viciously sharpened tongue...
Slut.
Skank.
Scrounger.
Fatty.
Who does it profit when a woman grinds another one down?
Distributing shame should never be a condiment...
and that ladder you clamber up so forcefully
should never be made of the leftover pieces
of people you have broken.
Sisters.
SISTERS.
Let that prescription for venom lapse.
File down those claws.
Pack away the hurdles, the flags, the glossy posters for the
pettiness race:
let's all quit,
let's all boycott

that performance.
A woman's heart is never indestructible, it never feels things differently
just because it's not yours
and scars still feel the pain,
still throb
long after they fade.

The Dreaded

A wisp,
a scent.
You turn your head.
Is something there?
Nothing but your imagination,
the rational asserts robustly,
and the unsettlement caused by the lateness of the hour,
the creaking of the roof,
the halting...steps.....?
A wisp,
a scent,
a fragrance borne upon the drafts of cold air seeping through
the chinks;
the unguarded,
the places no longer blocked by the stiffening of your neck.
Enter the dreaded,
while your mind trips over itself to win the race
and reassure.
Smooth your muscles locked into ironwood,
calm screaming nerves as denial pours patronizing honey to
slow its grappling hooks flung at your skin.
A wisp,
a scent.
The dreaded is with you,
upon you,
unseen
or unadmitted
and very hungry...
as cold tears trail down your spine.
Maybe if you don't look,
if you appear placid and unconcerned,
if you can uncurl your white knuckles,
unclench your abdomen,
maybe it will go

away,
or maybe
it never will,
because it has never really left you.
Perhaps the dreaded has been invited...
or perhaps
it is home.

Alone She Dances

Alone she dances,
always alone,
in an empty room of bare boards and peeling paint,
but surrounded in her head by an attentive,
adoring crowd.
Alone she dances,
lost in the movements,
her feet bleeding like a teabag in hot water,
prints like spilled wine tracking her endless brisés,
her graceless glissades,
while in her mind's eye the performance unspools like the most delicate of linen
and she knows she should stop daydreaming about her own death,
only so she can practice more fully its performance,
should stop praying for a faulty noose;
but, on a locked and hidden level, wonders if,
like a thistle in a kiss,
the pain is brief but the rewards exquisite;
and she dances on,
alone except for a pallid reflection in a battered mirror,
she dances….

Under the Winter Sky

The sky is winterfrosted and sharp
and, as you clatter down the stone steps,
something shimmering and white pulls your eyes and
in the dusk she stands.
She smiles
a smile of promise and the hunger of a thousand arctic nights
and of
love
of a kind;
but you are hard and helpless all at once and somehow get
through your maze of doors,
the keys tossed in a tiny clash of metal,
forgotten;
and the bed takes the collision in a bluish white glow of a
blizzard
and the stars are cold in her eyes and they reflect the stars
diamond bright against your back
and you are pierced with them,
between them,
until the light grows warm,
stills,
and the sheets are empty,
cooled flat by the press of unearthly flesh;
and you travel the streets with no desire for the sparkling
eyes
or the full,
too full,
rosy cheeks pouting at you.
Your stuttering heart and soul are given over to the perfection
of deathless ice forming on violet smudged lips,
the sheen of cold marble thighs;
and you smile to yourself
and the people who pass you recoil at your grin,

recover and shake off their brief vision of you astride a pale horse,
wearing a crown of horn ,
moonblinded and mighty;
and you throw your arms open to the north winds and laugh,
for they are shrieking,
calling you by name
and you stand panting and reckless and waiting
under the winter sky,
gazing up into the heart of the storm,
your blood freezing in anticipation
into crystals for you to lay at her feet.

In the Graveyard

"Respect ghosts and gods, but keep away from them." ~
Confucius

I stood in the graveyard and let the soil pour through my hands
and I felt naked
with only my grief wrapped around me,
hiding nothing;
and the birds called overhead and in my madness,
in my need,
I imagined they were cursing the ground I stood two-footed upon,
while I cursed them for being able to fly;
and for a heart that beat too fast to feel itself breaking
and I wondered how hard I needed to listen to hear you
sighing away from this place
and if the last sight of me stayed on surface of your eye
lingering like a too bright flashbulb
and if I pushed your eyelid up would I see myself
and does the dirt remember the bones that collapse into it
and do they merge together,
or is it like small ramshackle buildings crowding together,
tumbling against each other?
And I remember the last time I saw you not dying
and you laughed at something on TV and drank tea and there was no moment of clarity,
no clap of thunder,
no warning bell to tell me that this was it,
this was that moment,
the one I needed to have caught and kept in a silver box
with the dried flowers withering upon it.
And the birds still curse and I leave the sad space,
this mourning in rectangles
with all the stones poking up to mark where the ghosts begin

and I wonder if they see me walking away and try to follow, or if they want to stay

Strange Compass

"I have no right to call myself one who knows. I was one who seeks, and I still am, but I no longer seek in the stars or in books; I'm beginning to hear the teachings of my blood pulsing within me. My story isn't pleasant, it's not sweet and harmonious like the invented stories; it tastes of folly and bewilderment, of madness and dream, like the life of all people who no longer want to lie to themselves." ~ Herman Hesse, *Demian*

The road is mapped out for you matter-of-factly,
twined and braided into your umbilical cord
and you are fed instructions with your cereal;
but nobody tells you how those paths wind
and turn and twist
or disappear,
or that some may drop you into a pit...
Your blood will lead you, can speak to you,
but first you need to learn its language
and fear its messages
just a little,
for fiery blood carries all your pasts
as well as your present.
Can you bring that lodestone with you?
Can you cradle it,
bend without breaking under the weight?
Can you expand inside to absorb,
to imprint that compass rose across your lungs so that each
breath is magnetized...
to gather the lessons,
dropped like acorns across these bisecting roads?
To accept those as gifts,
even when they hurt?
Then believe.
Believe

and add your own footnotes to this unwritten tale,
add your footprint to the trackless
and add the calling of your blood
to that strange compass.
Toss a coin into the crossroads
and leave it lying unchecked in all its shiny wishfulness
as a beckoning.

Still Friends

You said that we would still be friends
and that nothing was really over,
but you spoke in a blank room of empty air
and those eyes,
those eyes never felt your words;
and I'm burning cold,
burning like bare hands scraping ice to grasp a frozen door handle.
You told me not to struggle,
that help was on the way
and to save myself from drowning would be faithless,
but left me to float
with no direction,
without solid ground in sight.
Hope was the unkindest crumb you threw me.
So I will go and buy a ticket
anywhere
rather than search for a mirage,
placing no reliance on
unheard prayers to a tin god
who leaves you with a hollowed heart
and promises like chalk drawings on a sidewalk
running in the rain
like I am now
with your stolen dice in my pocket.
The fix is in,
but I'm no longer gambling
on the game of "still friends".

Bella Donna

With scarcely a ripple she emerges from the river
and pauses on its muddy banks,
looking back in envy at the moon on the water,
wishing she could slow dance so close forever.
She weaves her wedding skirt of Spanish moss
and with magnolias laced into her hair
she goes searching for her bridegroom.
No shy maiden this:
she is a huntress, not the prey,
and the favored knight of revelry,
once chosen,
will beg to follow her,
to dine at her table and be fed with her own cool, white hands,
no hunger unfulfilled.
The moonlight follows grinning as
the damp night pulses with the stamp of feet and washboard rhythms,
beads and eyes glittering,
she drifts before him,
inviting and playfully leading
and, in dry-mouthed wanting, he trails after her.
"Welcome home cher..," she whispers
and the moon gives extra light
to their first dance and first kiss,
swaying among the silent houses standing sentinel
in the city of the dead;
and her nightshade scent envelopes him,
soothes and stirs him;
and the moon gazes down fondly...
Much later, she slips from his arms
and saunters through the gates
with a last loving look and a blown kiss
and he waits there eternally faithful,

bound to her as tightly
as the entwined jasmine vines.
She returns to the dank of the river,
waltzing a little on its muddy banks,
still reflecting the dancing moon
and the cypress trees rustle in a soft wind
as she sinks back,
murmuring,
into the water.

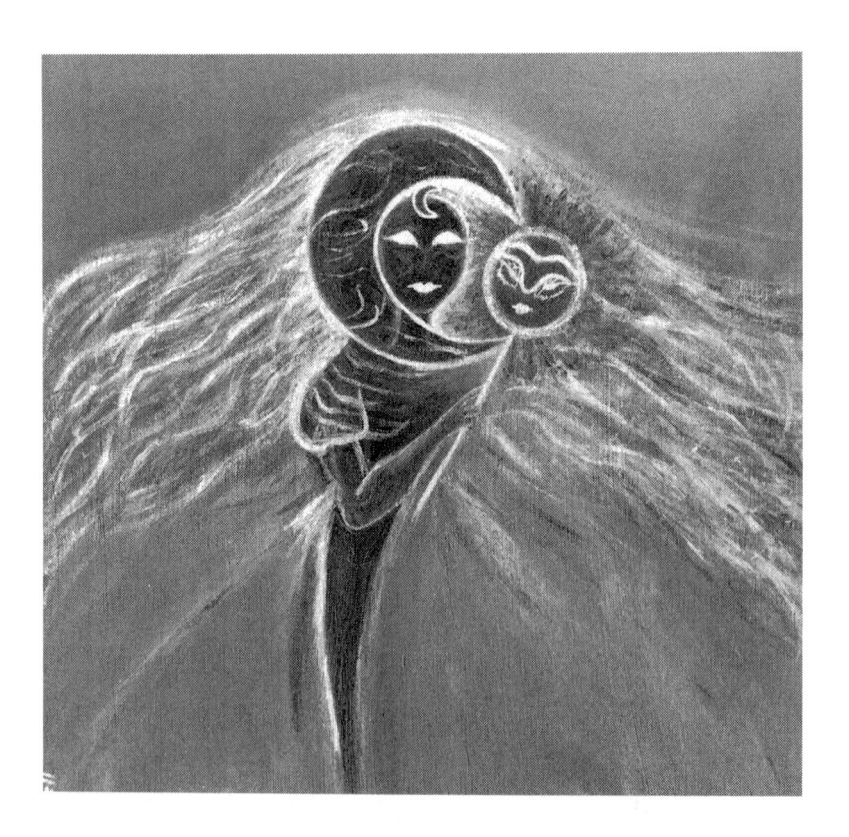

Static Days

Another morning walk to the train station
only to stand mannequin-like on the platform.
I feel the train approaching
and the wave of movement starts,
but I stay still,
letting the people break around me.
I don't go forward.
I don't go backward.
I am inert,
static,
and my mind has gone underground,
while the trains pass one after another...

I stand at the window
and listen to the hush breaking under the weight of the birds song
and gaze at the sunrise painting the sky;
and I should gather that gold into my arms
to carry through the day,
leaving light in the spaces I move through.
But all I feel is sunset.
I am sinking beneath the edge
and darkening
and there is only farewell in the music my heart beats in time with.

These are static days for me
and I am unchanging in a constantly changing world,
rigid and marking blind time,
waiting for something to move me.

The Bells

She delays the moment of rising,
of cover throw back and movement,
until she hears the church bells
ringing silver into the bland air of morning
and knows she can't stay any longer,
the dance of cold on bare floorboards and a murky mirror
reflecting a faded room and a fading face.
She knows shouldn't be there,
she knows she died once upon a time...
but there's nowhere else for her to go
and the memory of the bells,
even though rusted silent and green with moss,
is enough keep her rising.

Pleurant

Veiled Lady, cry for me,
spill your silent tears.
Let them pour like rain
to wash away any paltry memories.
Use them to feed the grass,
for I have no use for them any longer.
My lonely journey has finished
as solitary as it began.
There were no songs shared,
no laughter under starry skies,
no hands to clasp;
and none can touch me now.

Borders

You stand at the edge and look exactly where you have been
warned not to,
straight down;
and as the vertigo grabs you in a too-tight embrace.
You understand why people avoid gazing into the face of the
gorgon,
why they place such desperate faith in silver and painted
eyes,
why they keep their closet doors tight shut and their feet
tucked under the blanket;
because, for magic to be mastered,
it first must be faced.
All the layers of the universe demand order:
miss a step,
miss a line,
and the waiting ones who circle without ceasing,
who exult in a door freshly made in the underbelly of reality,
will swarm, pressing until it bulges like a bot fly ready to
emerge,
until the borders grow thin enough to tear.

You stand shuddering at the crossroad made visible for a
single flicker.
Sleight of hand and coins and rabbits
are the tawdry bastard children of the true,
the deep binding magic,
while illusion wavers siren-like in front of you.
The step you need to take is a small thing,
but your human spirit shrinks down,
as your eyes and the crabbing, creeping doubt join together
and you step back,
you step back
and leave it all behind.
You turn with purpose and stride away,

terror biting at your sensible heels,
the spell unbroken, untried,
unchallenged.
You settle for the safe and the sane
and the trifling...
Pages turn and later in a last, lucid moment you grasp at a fluttering thread,
a tattered corner of a dream, a fragment, a memory
and wish you'd had the strength,
the faith,
to willingly take that step, that small thing,
so long ago,
as time slows to a trickle and the sound of wings grows louder
a different type of magic approaches swiftly,
one which does not require your acquiescence, your discipline
or permission.
The final mystery
is upon you:
now you must take that step,
one step,
and cross the borders.

I Knew

The first time I saw you, my fingerprints had already
memorized what your cheekbones felt like,
curved like seaglass against the pillow,
and I already knew how you looked from behind when you
were standing in a slow line,
could see the impatience moving up redly in your neck;
and I knew that to make you laugh would cool the color back
down;
and that you thought brownies were good but coolwhip
straight from the container was better;
and I knew how your dreams twinged and poked you every
time you drove past the college you dropped out of;
and I loved you for the softness in your eyes as you watched
kids whirling by on a playground;
and I knew you would build a forever kind of fire in my heart
that crackled and smoked with your name and left your scent
in my hair;
and I knew you would leave me.
And so,
the first time I saw you,
I looked away
and counted one one thousand…two one thousand
until you disappeared;
and I knew I would miss you.

The Tunnel

Nobody can see,
there's no one to stop you.
Throw caution to the wind and buy a ticket,
even though it's one way only.
The tunnel beckons and the music drops the rhythms like breadcrumbs
and you follow,
shivering deliciously at the dark.
"Keep your arms and head inside the train at all times."
"Keep your head…"
And the night suddenly erupts in color and the scents of cotton candy and frying dough
and blood, sweat and
fears.
The mirrors only reflect outwards in here and you're suddenly glad you came,
because you're not in Kansas anymore;
you're in a place that's not possible,
not real.
Well, you never belonged in the real anyway,
because the spectres that walked through your nightmares stopped and told you,
told you
things;
and you listened,
wrapped in the comfort of the dark,
while, in the daylight, chattering hurt your head and made you dizzy,
like needles in your eyes and ears.
And those that dwell in the sun called you slow
and dumb.
But some roses only open in the dusk,
will only share their fragrance with the denizens of midnight,
the tribes of the moon;

and you are fully in their shade now,
as the train speeds up and the borders are melting
and the nightmares ride hellbent to meet you
and you know you have finally come
home.

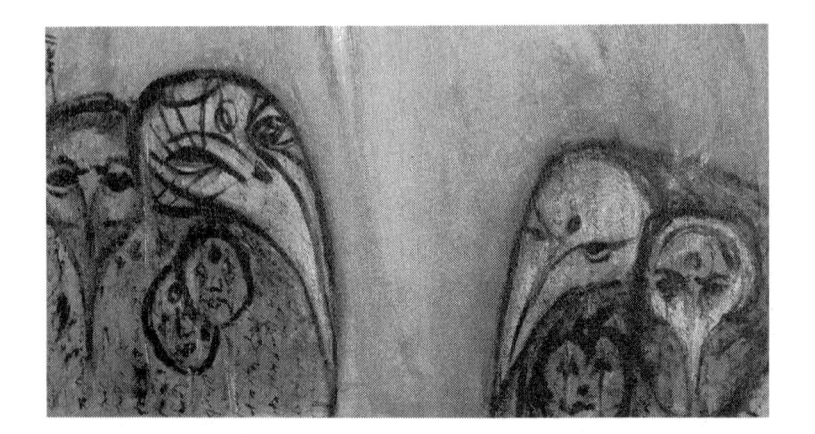

The Wonder Bus

Like a fork dragged across a china plate,
her voice cuts through,
creating a wavelike wince along the aisle.
My neck turtles in and I ignore her loudly,
turning to stare out the window as if a new territory was unfolding
instead of the same street,
same route
as the day before and before.
I wear my isolation like a large, black jewel,
a thing of sparkle without light,
and wonder if I am the only one so uncomfortable,
and wonder why I am;
and wonder why she isn't.
I guess bus rides make me ponder odd things.
With blank space to fill, strange thoughts rise up
like discarded rattles thrown on a floor for attention.
And I wonder if I am the only one who has these questions;
and wonder why I do;
and wonder why you don't.

Closets

I am hiding in a closet,
in a dark too big to get through,
sitting on a nest of crossed-out love poems
and sweaters
and books with broken spines.
The only sound is the hangers' ting
and the secret slide of moth wings against the wall.
And I let them nibble holes in me
until I am light enough
to find a way out.

Use Well the Day

Use well the day,
the long and short of it,
the dark and light
and all that's wedged squeaking in the in-between,
even the parts under the furniture where nobody sweeps.
Use well what time has handed you,
a present ,
a letter,
a map,
a faded photograph,
a match.
Use well the power,
your power,
your force.
Stride through the room all Annie Lennox-y
like you own it,
like you own yourself,
because you do.
And let them watch you in dismay,
in disdain,
in longing fawning,
in admiration;
and store that up,
bottle and cork it carefully
to use well
tomorrow.

Tatiana

White veils and a white room where the pianist played one-finger notes
that hung trembling in the sterile air,
while the silk boiled
and the white winds changed at every corner.
Poor lady,
sad Tanushka.
Little did you think that this place of blood and hard healing
would be your Rai.
Later, in the house of special purpose,
the white nights and whitewash would wear you down,
pare you to razor sharpness;
but even that would not save you,
for you had no skill in cutting,
no chance in fighting back.
The white women circled and pressed a cold kiss to your forehead,
sealing you,
marking you for their own,
while you sipped tea with delicate attention and let the steam caress your face,
the only one that would be allowed that liberty.
As the white nights rolled on and over like an army
leaving little trace on the frozen ground,
except for the few fallen sparrows which no one counted,
and some white tracks fading into slumps of ice
in that frightened uneven air.

I Soar Still

The crying didn't slow you,
the blood didn't stop you,
my pain didn't faze you.
Nothing could deter your ego-driven desire to make me ground-bound,
only fit for a dazed and creeping walker,
trailing behind you,
coughing at the dust you kicked up.
To soar higher you needed to build yourself
and I was your scaffold.
As I broke and cradled my torn wings,
my soul should have gasped and died;
and it did,
a little,
but you were not enough to break me forever,
not enough.
Steadily the force built, flamed;
and my resolve held me up and my arms pounded ceaselessly
until they brought forth in sweat and tears,
in black and blue magic,
new wings.
As I slipped them on and stepped to the precipice,
I left you crawling,
bawling after me
and counted:
one,
two,
three;
and welcomed the momentary oblivion
as the sky ushered me back into its embrace,
and cried joyful rain over and with me
and you;
crumbled back in thwarted impotent fury,
kicking into the dust you choked me with.

And I soared
and I soared
and I soar still.

The Song of Stars

It began when, as a child, you would lie in the grass
smelling the dark green of the night and look up
at the sky
and count the stars and call to them
in their own tongue
and then fall silent and listen hard,
listen deep,
above the whirring of wings and the many songs of the wind
to hear them as they answer.
"Sister,"
they named you
and you felt them inside you,
elusive,
like a vapor trail
you could follow but not touch.
But it was enough to know that you had stars pouring
through your veins
and your heart and your soul
whispering in your ears and shining in your eyes
and the sky taught you the words to join in the aria of blue
and green and shimmering life
created in other
far away night skies,
before time's hands started moving.
The ocean also spoke to you,
claimed you in water, blood and salt
and your very skin warmed in recognition.
For what is salt but tiny stars,
crystals with facets gleaming,
refracting and reliving
their lights and their world?
And those songs are smaller, but the whole universe fits
inside
and you feel them overflowing

as the light spills from you;
and the flickers of your fingers in the air
call the fireflies to you,
for they too
recall and reverence the stars.

Ghost Writing

I dipped my pen and wrote with ink distilled from my marrow
and the words writhed and smoked upon the page;
and where it touched me
my hand was burned.
I wrote from half-remembered dreams of childhood and wishes upon long-exploded stars,
but the ink was watercolor pale and melted away, clinging briefly to the edges and then…
gone.
My nightmare thoughts made black smears over the paper,
but didn't spell out the words,
only hinted dreadful things and then changed when I tried to look closer,
shifting into another language;
and I was exhausted from the work
and the pages were bellowing for me to fill them.
So I penned a sigh
and a memory
and they softened and quieted
and then I wrote your name.

Naming Makes You Real

You kissed me and it hurt,
but I was supposed to smile and thank you
and keep the bruises hidden like they were a defect,
because hurting me was too much entertainment to stop only
because of my tender skin,
with shameful names assigned at random and words like weapons,
like stones thrown at a target who had nowhere to move.
It was so easy to convince me I was wrong for doing none of
the things you accused me of,
but I found myself guilty
and sentenced to hard solitary.
It was easier to be with the friends who were invisible,
because they never asked the hard questions
and when you left with her
it never occurred to me that it wasn't my fault.
I understand why you have to say your name in AA.
It means something when you say who you are.
Naming makes you real.
The words spoken take shape and draw first breath as they
leave yours.
I should practise saying my name into the wind,
saying it until it fits in my mouth instead of spitting it out
awkwardly.
I should practise having a conversation without flinching,
try not to worry what expression my face should be
modeling;
and if I can ever let myself care,
because it's so hard to re-learn feeling when
your soft heart has been triple-wrapped in brown paper and
packed away,
and the tears I wouldn't cry
have hardened like sap into amber.
But maybe that's all that's holding the jagged edges together

and my spaces would be so empty without the discarded
pieces
and counterfeit promises
and the map to the places where my mind hid my secret
longing
for something else,
something far away,
stuffed like newspapers to stop the drafts in an old house.
The box I just dragged out to the curb with the trash
couldn't possibly hold it all.
But I know what's real now
and I know my name
and one day soon
I will claim it.

Spots On the Sun

I stand in the sun but the warmth moves away,
leaves me in blank spots.
I seem only to curl up in the places the light shies away from
and keeping warm is now a phantom,
a wishing, a memory.
My soul shivers and, as my hands touch the mirror,
I watch my pale face frost over,
wavery and indistinct.
I bundle into all the wool and down I can carry with me,
but it soon catches the cold and holds it
damply against my chest and seeping into my feet.
The heat promised crawls away,
overwhelmed.
I press my cheeks against the walls and think
I am like an old stove long-emptied of wood or paper which
now stands silently
chilled and weeping rust.
There are spots on the sun and I live in those,
a captive to the shadow,
a stunted pale green shoot,
curling away from the cold and into myself
and dreaming of the sunshine,
of crackling sparks
and bricks made warm in the light.

Perceptions

"*There are things known and there are things unknown, and in between are the doors of perception.*" ~ Aldous Huxley

The water was endless and she cleaved through it with practised movements,
flipping over to gaze at the dome of the sky,
the clouds in their everchanging shapes undulating,
dripping their shadows across her damp face;
and she lifted a hand in greeting
as if acknowledging a friend,
wondering what it felt like to be high and to ride the wind.

The air above the clouds was full of light and the wind currents of hot and cold
met and danced;
and the sky opened back and back,
unfolding the heavens.
She hung over the side and gazed at the swelling and roll of the waves,
squinting against the diamond spray,
and wondered what water felt like
as it coated your body and if you bobbed like a cork or sank like a stone.
And she held her hand out before her as the wind split around it
and dreamed about the mysteries of the deep and of conquering the tides.

Deep and silent, dark as sable, the tunnel cradled and surrounded her
as she poked her nose upward toward the gleaming tendrils of light.
Eyes tight-shut against the merciless brightness which seeped down into the cool earth,

she stood in the stillness feeling the murmur of soft and growing soil,
listening as the tunnellers gathered
to hear and share stories,
fables about a place with no ceiling,
with nothing to anchor them to ground and a glaring star
which nothing on the surface could escape.
And she wondered
what it was like to stand upright and alone
with nothing but emptiness stretching around and above her
and what it would be like to
see her own face.

Three separate souls reach out in curiosity and longed-for wonderment,
three hearts beating out the same song,
the same craving in unison,
but each deaf to the rhythm of the others,
like echoes bouncing off of distant cliffs
only to fade.

Who Will Help Me Carry Him?

My arms are strong but the sorrow weighs more with each mile
and my heart adds heaviness to every step.
The whimpers of the ones I pass by nick me like scalpel flashes,
but I dare not slow down,
cannot falter,
or I will never start again
and risk becoming a pile of shapeless rags blowing weakly
on the side of the road,
obscured by hot dust the color of mustard.
Who will help me carry him?
Who will lend their muscles, their hands and feet,
their sweat
and walk down this road
with hands cupped to catch,
not to push away?
Who will speak for him,
to lend a voice to the voiceless,
to raise the volume until the wax melts from the ears of the insulated,
the deliberately,
persistently
unaware?
He has no name,
his only signature the dried blood under his nose;
and he will never thank you,
but your arms will remember the weight
and your eyes will reach back and call the color of that blistered sunrise
to mind,
and your ribs will catch,
will hitch,
with a memory-ache of that bruising.

Empty prayers and promises echo like old cans knocked off a tree limb,
tinny and harsh;
and flowing prose on clean white paper a lifetime away is no currency here.
Who will help me carry him?

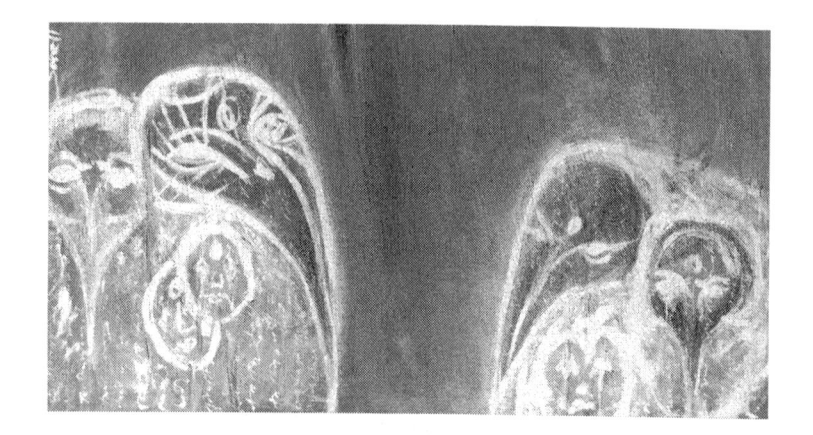

On a Train

I can't hear the music but my feet can feel the beat
and, though I avoid looking at anyone, I know what they all
are wearing;
and my heart is clacking time with the tracks,
and I feel myself getting smaller as the distance grows,
being pulled, stretching like taffy;
and I listen for the snap.
I imagine everyone who is running feels like this,
second-guesses screaming your name;
but the sky is reaching down and I want to hitch that ride.
And if the baggage you can't see is heavier than the faded
one I'm carrying,
let me pretend I am handling it,
let me pretend all I feel is nonchalantly strong,
while I keep my face blank and badass
as the landscape blurs and changes
and I can taste the strangeness in the air.
My restless feet stumbling over each other,
twitching to get walking
and leave the track behind.

I'm On A Train For Somewhere

I'm on a train for somewhere,
sandwiches and good wishes in my new old bag
and I try not to be afraid,
because I have done nothing wrong;
but that won't save me if the wrong arms reach out to grab me.
Speaking in tongues, I look anywhere but into a face,
because that may set the fuse sizzling and I keep trying to run from explosions.
I'm on a train for somewhere:
it's supposed to be so simple;
but simple people are the ones who can disappear easily.
You need to be complex to grow defenses,
to have an explanation that will open ears instead of making them cringe,
or jeer,
or check their wallets.
I'm on a train for somewhere
and my eyes won't heed my orders not to cry
and the kindness that I stumbled into for a while
can't touch me here,
can't warm me here.
I know how children feel when the shadow monsters crawl out
and a frightened scream only brings a "Shhhhhhh, it will be alright."
Will it?
If you haven't seen the monsters,
how do you know how to fight them?
How do you know if they're really gone?
They are masters at lurking, at the careful construction of their snares,
and oh so patient.
I'm on a train for somewhere

and the streets are like a maze of mirrors.
Everywhere you turn
you are back where you started;
and I want to flee this cockroach existence,
but fear has me in its merciless bony-fingered grasp.
I'm on a train,
I'm on a train.
I hope it never stops.

A Deep Blue Lovesong

If I touch my lips to your wrist can I feel the rise and fall,
like the waves of the ocean,
because there is a tidal pull in you and I hear it
when I press you to my ear.
Like water, you pull the light from the moon and glow with it
and as long as I can follow that shimmer, I will never get lost.
Soft like sand and water,
soft like sea foam wings,
and the brush against my skin feels like it's leaving stars in its wake;
a trail to navigate by at night.
And a silvery kind of song rises in my throat, caught and flashing,
but even if the words won't surface,
I can hum it to you,
while I touch my lips to your wrist once more.

Building Dreams

Dreams come and go
and sometimes they stay and get to know me for awhile,
rustling in the night and sharing a secret joke.
Sometimes they come with a glare and a slap
or a pinch,
sharp and angry,
and exit dramatically like a summer storm.
I add characters and settings
and other times
most times
change the words.
I carry them with me everywhere and escape into them as often as I can,
because I much prefer that world to this one.
I toss their pebbles into the water and watch where the ripples go
and I follow,
casting spider threads across
to build a bridge of silk
for the dainty feet of visions to pass.
Dreams come and go
and I splash them with the colors of their emotions
and the deepest dark ones I try to surround with light;
but sometimes I am too full of dark myself
to spare any…

Headaches

"I have a headache," he tells her peevishly,
and she scurries to find the plastic bottle of "medicine"
and a glass of water.
He doesn't thank her, just groans and stretches with bleared
eyes and breath curling out of him like something left too
long dead in the august sun.
Stale odors rise from the clothes strewn across the floor and
crumpled bits of paper,
phone numbers he doesn't bother to hide.
Breakfast is served in a room packed tight with silent
screams
stretching on and on,
until he is satisfied with her cowering
and with all the lordly dishes brought before him.
She doesn't cry or question, just keeps well out of arms reach
until the shower stops
and she brings him his towel.
She also brings, unasked for,
a hammer
and a long spike,
pulled with desperate consideration from a fence in the
spring sunshine
many months,
many bruises,
many humiliations ago.
She cures his headache
once and for all time
and sits in the now truly silent room,
her face a blank wall,
waiting to be told what she should do next,
gently rubbing
her aching head.

Telling Truths

If I should sit down uninvited
near your table
and you feel my eyes licking your face,
will you wonder what this forward woman
is doing,
while a polite and correct smile struggles to fit itself to your mouth?
And if I should tell you that I write
and that I write truthful things,
but get confused and tangled in the inconstancy of it,
and gaze at you beseechingly,
pleading without words,
would you know what I was saying?
Or would you gulp your coffee
nod coldly and walk swiftly to the door?
I write the truth as it is mine to write,
a story of a tunnel with no beginning,
no finish,
a spiral.
There are false stops that announce the end,
but there is always a hidden door, an unmarked passage;
and the tunnel lopes away like a bolt of grey cloth
rolling unchecked.
If I should tell you these things
while holding a glass of wine and leaning in too close
to study the flecks in your eyes,
while trying to explain the Russian doll of emotions I am made of,
would you perhaps nod in grateful acknowledgement,
in solidarity?
Or would the bedroom be your focus, your destination,
the wine brimming in my glass your vehicle.
The paper before me is a mirror but the view from every angle changes

like the seasons,
sometimes frozen and at another glance new growth or strange forms appear.
My truth demands I put this down,
the theme running through this endless tunnel,
this book of lives,
of my intersections and full stops,
of tears and hopeful hands that still remember how to reach.
And all the times I pause and blunder into another who looks like they may have seen the same visions,
who may also try to decipher this poetry of knots
with the same devotion and loathing that I do,
I reach out....I try to build a bridge with the tools I have,
the things I think are solid and unchanging.
But everything changes.
The words I speak never measure up to the written
and I am defeated once again,
diminished somehow by the asking.
And they always let walk away.

If I should find you,
if I should find you in your own search.
If we should see each other,
read each other,
would that tunnel accommodate us in our walk together?
Would that truth become large enough for two,
or maybe our combined strength would be enough to hold it down,
to keep the Manitou from shifting,
To see one, single vision in the mirror.
And if I should write that,
would it be beautiful?
So beautiful...
Or would the telling crack it forever?

The Toy Shop

The toy shop door shuts with a final bang and snicking of the locks:
snick one,
snick two,
snick three
and...
done.
For a while, all is still and silent,
while the rushing footsteps and the traffic sounds outside settle,
are muted through the walls
like cheesecloth straining the sharpness,
dulling the edges and tamping down the clatter.
And soon the noise and light fade.

The room stands ready,
like a giant in drawn breath,
and smoothly,
without fanfare,
there is purposeful movement
and eyes blink,
painted ones and glass ones and button ones:
blink once,
blink twice,
blink three times
and...
all clear.
A dance of sorts.
A song of sorts.
A meeting of sorts.
More details I cannot give.
But marionettes are the royalty in this shop
and the fat and the stuffed and the carved all adore their flashing strings,

their prancing, rhythmic limbs.
Dreams and legends of light are told and retold and marveled at,
like marbles to the eye they imagine swirls of color and
bubbles caught forever,
suspended in bright air.
All too soon the sun's emissary moves closer,
seeping apricot into the ebony
and, like a hive after winter,
slowly the hum and movement rise from the street;
while inside, just the opposite,
the last twirl,
the last notes,
the last tale,
as whatever enchantment briefly ensouls this place of small
and gentle magic
dissolves.
And later,
when the door is unlocked and the shades rattled up,
a single, unseen, roving eye may turn toward the light
just a quick superstitious glance,
drawn by fear and fascination:
blink once,
blink twice,
blink.

Silver Coins

I travel through this day
counting the hours,
the minutes
and all the spaces in between.
And against the background of my living is the sound,
the faraway chink,
of silver coins dropping.
I will betray you with a kiss and never lose sleep,
while gazing at my awards and moving in circles closed tight
to those who will not fall,
will not bend.
An opulent window-dressing the only landscape I crave, to
walk wrapped in neon warmth,
and if the shrivelling behind my ribs twinges, I can ignore it.
I have ignored much more.
All will fade and the deepest cut is the only scar that remains
silver.
I count no tomorrow,
no higher plane,
and my only steadfast companion,
the only constant,
is that faraway music of the coins.

Seeing

See me.
Look at me.
You already have, you say.
a hundred times, you say.
Then tell me,
what color do my eyes turn when I am sad,
when I am angry?
Does the rising color in my cheeks offend you?
Can you see me?
Can I matter?
Or, like marching ants along a sidewalk,
will you step over me,
past me,
with nothing to hold your interest,
nothing stirring you to look once,
twice.
A mere chain of identical segments,
but not a single one with a name.
Nobody you recognize.
See me,
look at me.
At me,
at the woman, not an 8 x 10 flat photo dusted once a week.
Not the girl in your mind's eye that you were introduced to
long ago in a noisy room,
who filled a checklist of necessary qualifications so
efficiently
that no further research was required.
File closed.
You never invited me to swim into the deep end with you,
floating in the shallows was sufficient;
and there were many other interests to be explored
and machinations to tinker with that were more intriguing
than

this face.
See me,
see into me,
and let me look back,
long and unguarded.
Let me drink my fill.
I have been thirsty for so long.
Let me blow a kiss,
like a dandelion wish,
floating across our shared breath and we could inhale together
that first taste of possibilities,
that subtle perfume of nascent trust.
See me,
sun full on my face and hair unpinned and windwild,
nothing standing between your eyes and mine.
I'm scared,
but I will hold very still and give you time to pause and perhaps
stay a while.
See me,
seeing you.

Shadow Touch

You saw me a thousand times but never actually knew I was there.
You walked past me,
shared buses and libraries and an occasional lecture;
but you never saw me,
never looked at me in a way that stopped and hooked your eyes into
noticing,
like a blurred photo sharpened.
And I,
I never stepped out from the bland safety of the background.
I never tried to hold your eyes with a smile or a gesture.
Perhaps, if I'd put on a layer of protective face paint and hid behind large glasses
and played music,
you may have dropped a quarter in my hat
and looked
with a curiosity about what was really there;
and, in that moment,
more than just our shadows may have touched.
But I never did and you never did and there was no fault.
It's just the way of the solitary heart.
To be surrounded and unable to trust,
never to collect enough courage to tear free of the background,
never to send anything except your shadow
out to touch.

Searching For A Lamp

You weren't wanted,
as far as your eye could see;
a cold, lonely future stretching into the long unknown.
So you protectively
burrowed into a far place,
only to find
a chance,
a slender, saffron thread,
that perhaps you were wrong.
But too late…
Now the escape tunnel is shuddering,
ready to collapse,
and your window of opportunity is shrinking.
Soon you won't be wanted again
and despair burrows its way under your skin, chasing away
all the heat,
the life,
like water dripped,
sizzling on to a hot griddle.
And you reach for that blanket of hope
to try and warm yourself again
and peer once more into that lonely landscape
searching for a lamp,
a light,
a flicker,
bursting against that unbroken empty space;
but only silence meets your eyes.

The Best Days of My Life

The parties I wasn't invited to,
the boy who kissed me and then laughed about it to his friends,
the time my period arrived early and stained my jeans in school,
the jokes I never understood,
the cool I never felt,
the stumbling fumbling I always managed in gym.
And forty years later,
my cheeks still flood with color
and my stomach still remembers.
These were supposed to be the best days of my life.
All I could see was an endless track of nowhere to hide,
no place to turn;
and the best advice my mother naively offered was, "Smile and be friendly…"
You can't be invisible and smile.
Impossible to be friendly while the vicious fledglings crowd around you,
jeering and pointing at the outfit you briefly,
wrongly,
felt pretty in.
When the only thing faster than their tongues was their fists
and the shame of just being,
of being Me,
was more weight than I could bear.
And forty years later,
my cheeks still flood with color
and my stomach still remembers
the best days of my life.

Shifting Shadows

Shifting names,
shifting natures,
shifting and unbalanced to the sluggish surface eye perhaps,
because those eyes are the easiest to deceive.
The wheel turns too swiftly
to see how the clay forms,
emerging from its gob of swamp matter,
hands sunk to wrists in the birthing.
There is no true shifting, just the accepted perception
crackling along your throat,
up your neck,
the groping towards feeling what words will work,
will form the shapes that open doors,
will roll the stone away.
This is my story,
this is my song.
I may compare it to living in a house with shadow cats,
tantalizing and elusive in their devotion.
To catch a clear glimpse one must use other eyes,
for all glasses in here are seen through darkly
and images swirl,
like hot wax in standing water.
But my heart has become a chamber of midnight where the
light only confuses
and I pad silently with the cats,
staying in the corners,
embracing the shadows,
learning them,
as the shapes I need to follow,
to give weight and form to the ink I breathe.
This is my story,
this is my song.
A story of the not-quite-seen
of the silvery flashes in deep water,

of the curtains moving
that stop when your eyes catch.
A song of the under,
the sideways,
the long ago and the moment before,
a puzzle of infinite compositions.
A featureless land,
the end of the road,
where we shall meet in a place without any darkness
and break all the pots thrown on a wheel,
which kept spinning
long after the clay had run out.
This my story,
this is my song.
Yes, this is MY song
and my voice is the one that shifts,
that breaks and seizes tight from emotions hitting against the
jagged shoreline
I have tried to build dams next to;
and in that space,
that quiet space,
the shadows gather and cavort once more,
certain of their welcome,
certain of their place in the grey light,
that may be seen
or unseen as my capricious,
fractured,
shifting
will chooses.
And so, once more, I settle in here
like dust,
like smoke,
like shifting light.
This is my story,
this is my song.

Glue

I have sat for long days and longer nights listening to
the same music playing sorrow over and over in another
room,
a violin,
a cello,
pouring the sounds and sadness and soaring yearning into my
deliberate being.
Being still,
being careful.
Patiently gluing myself back together with tears and spit and
prayers and resolute no last looks.
And the death throes of dreams.
Sometimes I apply it with tiny, feathery brushstrokes
and other times pour straight from the pot,
letting it coat the ragged edges.
The seams match pretty well and in the evening or by
flickering candles you can hardly tell.
But, in the bright sunlight,
you can clearly see the tiny chips, can follow the shoreline of
cracks.
I don't mind:
I have become my own work of art,
my own ledger of experience and a testimony to the triumph
of a mighty spirit.
A soft heart can absorb sudden impacts and cushion even the
sharpest crash.
It weeps its own blood but grows stronger on it.
I have become a landscape, not of smooth sameness,
but of sloping dips and curves,
hidden places,
high spots and textures.
I stand facing the day with the shades up and the bright lights
full on.
If you see the ripples and

bumps and think to downgrade me,
to discount or shame me,
well, more fool you...
Because I have been tested and tried and still come back.
I have taken what was thrown,
staggered a bit it's true.
It took a few steps before I got my balance,
and yet I am still here.
If that offends you then look the other way,
keep to the shadows and veils of gauze and let your eyes linger only over the views which run unhindered, in smooth lines.
I won't be broken again, not in the ways that matter.
My glue is strong and the music has finally changed.

In the Midnight Garden

In the garden,
in the pewter-tinted evening,
moved by melancholy,
by nameless yearnings and the dying of the light
I walk.
I am brimming full of strangeness and dark
until they spill over, soaking and dragging at me,
the heaviness overwhelming and
I cannot stand upright,
cannot carry it any farther.
And if I fell to the ground and poured out all my passion and
pain and bewilderment
right there into the cooling grass,
would I feel release?
Would the earth accept it?
And what strange fruit would grow,
would be born out of this soul slurry, this morass of feelings
defying definition?
And if it were pressed and served to you in a clear and
ringing glass,
would you drink
this wine of madness,
of power and powerlessness?
This strangewine sown and watered with the inscrutable,
all spun by a vision,
a walk
in this midnight garden.

Medusan Dreams

It used to help to walk,
to wash the dishes,
to drive across lanes automatically checking for followers,
to paint my nails;
any movement pierced the green darkness shrouding my
minds eye and
turning the bright daytime world into murky scenes from an
old nightmare.
I became so practised in not talking about the things I knew,
because flowers growing from a skull so pale and venomous
have no place under electric lights.
But my tricks have finally worn through like fraying lace and
I stagger into the bathroom,
shuddering already with knowledge,
as the mirror shows me what I did not want to see:
a face the color of old dust and the flickering tongues and
glittering eyes of an unholy halo
fitted,
gifted
to me by a madness too big to measure
unless you drown in it first.
I heard a clock chiming but I couldn't tell when.
It's all a blur and I feel I have had this conversation with
myself before
and I am so dry with fear even the sweat has fled from me.
The truth hovers teasingly out of my reach
and I am too tired to jump for it;
so I sink on to the tile and lay my hissing head down,
one last rest before
I step off into the un-measurable.

The Color of Heartbreak is Yellow

Simple yellow dandelions
the color of butter,
of sunshine,
of crayons,
vibrant weeds hung heavily with childhood memories,
a caught beam of light
waiting to explode in wishes traveling on the wind.
And she picked them in a pretty bunch to lay across the lap
of the returned one
as a gesture,
a token
of her unchanging love.
A river bends and slows but always,
always,
the water moves and loves the sky it sparkles under and holds
the path gently,
even when it's crumbling and falling away and chokes the
river.
Empty words sprinkled like rain,
like tears,
and even emptier hands now fall to her sides
and she stands mutely screaming,
a wrenching cry out and into the universe:
"Why am I not loved?
Why am I not enough?"
And the universe swallows it
and answers,
"You are,
you're not,
everyone but you,
no,
not now,
too late,
of course my dear child,

not you not you not you."
But the screams echo,
clanging,
lodged too loud and tight in her ears to hear the answers,
while her bouquet of dandelions
wilts on the curb
where she tossed them,
hating the sight of them now,
shamed and misfitting,
unwelcome even in the smallest of burrows.
Sometimes the color of heartbreak is yellow.
Sometimes the river cries but nobody can see the tears for the water.
Sometimes letting go means you never,
ever
will.

Break the Sky

I am wrapped in silence,
in smoke and in manifest,
arrogant secrecy.
The dark shading my vision and coating my tongue with
waxy compliance,
eyes veiled and my hands gripped in place,
held fast with the strength of tree roots in splintered coldness.
And my brightness,
my light,
becomes an apparition,
a brief surfacing spray of memory,
a fading caress,
so promising,
so warm,
before deepening into the escape of sleep.
Perhaps Morpheus heard my formless,
my unspoken pleas,
and graced me with a fertile fragment of illumination.
For there is something still clinging,
flushed and quietly inside me,
my star still shining,
but softly
softly,
learning to test the locks and chains,
seeking out the fissures slowly expanding in the drought.
And I feel the warmth growing,
gathering the strength,
the courage,
the right;
and I will burst forth.
I will be the sun itself
and break the very sky.

Burning Call

"I desire the things that will destroy me in the end."
~ Sylvia Plath

Delicate glints of gold and platinum bubble as I tilt the
crystal goblet towards my lips,
eyes lidded,
marking the small deathwash against the glass,
as the stem captures the heat from my fingers and draws it
into itself,
magnifying,
igniting.
So beautiful, this flute of sparkling poison,
and I raise it,
toasting myself,
for I crave the burning,
the spreading conflagration inside.
All burnings call to me
with a hot and raging song,
out-of-control fire is where I want to crest.
To be seen against the glare and rising from the smoke like a
badgirl Venus,
riding the heat as if surfing an ocean wave.
I feed like wildfire
eating everything in my path and leave behind only my
initials
sweating in the steam.
My desire is for the dark,
the forbidden,
the dangerous,
that twilight walk along a slippery precipice,
the apple bitten,
not just once,
but eaten core and all.
And in the end,

the burning will be grand and glorious,
a crescendo of sparks and smoke.
And in the end,
I finally understand that Frankenstein loved his monster.
And in the end,
before the final sip,
the final flame,
the final step,
I will know that I have stood toe-to-toe,
breath-to-breath,
with dragons
and did not flinch.

Awful Like Me

The hated thing that dances,
raging,
and bares its teeth at old people,
slow people,
babies that cry and family members that will (prattle) phone all the time.
And it slithers through your brain,
leaving trails you scrub with frenzied denial:
not me not me not...
mine.
Private, deep moments worry-wondering if there is anyone else,
and does anyone else know about...
me.
Can they tell?
Do I wear it like stigmata,
like a camp number on my arm?
Do we all house monsters?
Do we all provide demons a waiting shoulder to perch,
skittering and landing with a whomp.
Wings wafting a stench of uncharity,
impatience,
selfishness
up your nose.
I must be the only one.
Nobody else is,
nobody else could possibly be,
awful
like me.

Machinery of Lost Memories

Where are the memories made that aren't kept?
What fantastical machinery constructs them,
fashions from newly-grown tendrils
or strands of a past time and place
and stamps them;
no longer needed,
displaced,
inferior?
Where are these cancelled ones?
I made them and lost them and sometimes I gaze at a
fragment,
run my thumb over it and remember,
just for a moment.
It would have been so easy to pass by her,
to miss her in the greyness of the rain and the fading light,
to avert eyes in a kind of muddled panicky "Don't know how
to if I should stop is it safe don't know just keep walking"
way,
the city sidewalk reaction we are all schooled in
unconsciously.
But the way she sat slowed me,
with her silent face raised to the sky,
as if she was waiting for the drenching
to douse the fire within her.
Was it mist or steam shimmering from her skin?
And I half held out my hand
and let it hang there for long seconds,
clumsy in the wet and with my bangs hung over my eyes.
I don't know if she saw me;
but the fever in her eyes gleamed red and hot
like banked coals
and, even after I walked away,
their light hung in front of me like the residue after a camera
flash.

And I felt her steam cooling as it rose from my hand and thinned,
disappearing into the machinery of lost memories.
The rain closed in around me as I kept walking.

A Song of Separation

"*Listen to the reed and the tale it tells, how it sings of separation..*" ~ Rumi, *The Reed Flute's Song or Mathnawi of Maulana*

The fall didn't kill her but the cold and the fright almost did
and no matter how fiercely she concentrated
her light stayed dimmed.
Blown out by the speed and the wind of her plummet,
she supposed,
her simple cupful mind only knowing the dark and the light,
the black and the white,
and that she was alone,
her reed broken and singing sadly of its separation.
Why she fell was anyone's guess,
but her gleaming siblings glimmered at her
and sent her hope that she would join them again soon,
strewn across the galaxy,
holding the blackness pinned back with points of diamond
and smiling gently as the wishes floated up and burst against
them like bubbles.
She never gazed into the monster's eye, never stared into the
abyss,
because she was both
and the becoming had stopped so long ago that memory
couldn't reach that far.
All was fully grown and fitted comfortably,
the sharp-bladed light not piercing any longer,
merely surrounding and filling in the rips and tears
the gaps where the other skies spilled over.
At first, she thought the earth was swelling,
growing like a rampant mushroom,
but the winds moved only past,
not with her,
and down she dropped,

straight like an acorn,
heavy like a drop of molten solder;
and the strange solidness would not yield and
gravity then proved its existence with a
clanging,
jarring,
pressing,
like a quilt made of lead.
The fast-fleeting winds caressed her hair once more,
kissed her and said good bye.
But it was a long, aching time before she could bear to look anywhere else
but up.

Dreaming Of Atlantis

You leap awake,
startled,
surprised you are in a bed
and your hands are stretched out,
ready to grasp.
What is this thing you are seeking
even in your deepest sleep?
This will o' the wisp
that evades you,
turns the corner seconds before you,
that vanishes into the trees?
As you pad through the woken day, is there a feeling tucked
into the corner of you,
a shadowed one that the broom keeps slipping over,
a feeling of longing
of missing,
of listening hard for something,
a stillness under your heartbeat?
Is it a ghostly twin
that your soul searches for
and your fancy gives a name;
a totem of a special flower or fragrance?
If I am reaching,
always reaching,
is it for a door?
A key?
The arm of my beloved?
Or is there a window I am rushing towards,
a last goodbye to call,
a last glimpse of sunrise?
Or maybe rocks to shatter across?
Am I dreaming of Atlantis
or of Valhallan Halls?
Of myself in old and new places?

I seem to miss things I cannot see or touch or name,
but they settle into my pillow and whisper
"Almost....almost..."
Science would dismiss it as a subconscious twitch,
an imprint,
a memory,
like seashells hiding in the desert dust.
Perhaps I am like the walls in a cave with paintings masked
under newer skins of stone.
If I continue reaching,
and my hands are suddenly caught and clasped,
will they be filled with dreams?
Or is that elusive
thing
I am searching for
something which can never be found?
If we could hold it, cup it in our hands warming and gazing
unhurried,
unobstructed,
would we evolve, would we move closer to a higher
understanding?
Would we find the glittering magic we have been missing,
like gilt worn away by greedy thumbs?
Or have we eaten too often on the insane root that Will
crooned about.
Are we like dreams of flying which end in a bed-sheet-
clutching crash?
For wings are fragile things and sometimes we rise,
we soar,
dipping and dancing like kites;
but mostly the wax just melts.
Do you ever reach out in this mid-space between awake and
wandering too,
with your hands surprised at their emptiness

and the blandness settling over your face like dust as you
recognize the walls of daytime and hear the cursed alarm
clock?
Do we dream of Atlantis?
Do we dream of Heaven?
Or is our shadow self signaling,
trying to help our corporeal,
our burdened and earthlocked, woken self
make its escape.

She

He writes of her in every gesture, with every motion,
in song,
in poetry,
carved in birdwing letters on stone,
on parchment,
in the sand.
He paints her on chipped and crumbling walls
and on flawless canvas,
on the backs of beetles and on the backs of his hands.
Stars and moon and raging tempests,
dying seasons and sunrise,
all telling the same tale.
She,
of the day and the dawning,
the night and the hidden.
Always
She,
whose name will never be forgotten,
is never spoken,
who is seen in every sleepy smile of a drowsing infant,
in every tear and in blood and in the scattered cooling ashes
of the dead.
She,
standing at once in light and impenetrable shadow,
raising palest arms in benediction.
And he writes her,
writes her,
sometimes weeping,
sometime praying,
but always writing,
reverencing,
remembering.
She.

Certain

You are leaving, you say,
because you cannot be certain
of anything here with me.
I wear both the Good Guy white hat and the Dastardly
Villain black one
and my actions do not always fit the time.
The trip and fall is never expected and no matter how
researched and high-rated the road,
a crater may open at any moment and that newborn abyss has
no map.
I know you have tried.
What you couldn't see was that I was trying too,
just not in the same way,
not in the approved Ann-Landers-advice way.
But we all fight battles
and sometimes the bloodiest ones are fought in silence.
I wish you well.
Of that,
I am certain.

I Never Should Have Followed

I never should have followed her;
but I did.
Catching one glint from her topaz eyes was the snare,
purposeful steps leading down and down,
around and through, not quite touching anyone.
And I followed her
to the river edge,
flowing sullenly under a weed-choked bridge of arches.
Night-time scent of animals, age and garbage:
Count the pillars: five, six...
The seventh was crumbling into the darkwater, it edges
chewed not worn.
A wooden door pitted with damp wedged open against a
slumped pile of dirt and sand and nameless bits,
trapped in trailing roots.
And I followed her.
In the darkness, no senses helped me.
I stumbled through passages, eyes blind, arms outstretched,
listening for a muted step.
And I followed her.
In that tenebrous place, there was no warning.
I was alone and then she was upon me
in a nightmare sound of ragged (wings) cloak.
"You should not have followed me..."
I know.
And then those topaz eyes turned full open,
spindle shaped and deep;
and she told me
of the library of things lost,
things best forgotten,
their tales of old etched in bones,
worn ivory and smooth with handling.
Chains and locks hold back the chitinous clatter of claws,
a spill of garnet, a scent of iron;

and the librarian (guardian) wanders among them,
ever vigilant.
The library of things lost
that need to stay lost,
stay forgotten.
I never should have followed her...
but I did;
and now I stay.

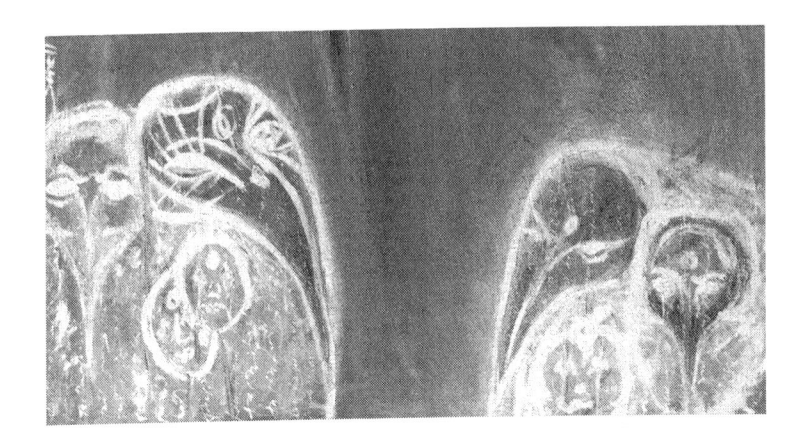

Mirror Dancing

We dance to endless music,
sometimes floating as lightly as web strands,
as dust motes pirouetting in a beam of sun;
other times in pounding floorshaking
to match the drumming in our pulse.
Feet and crimson passion keep the time as
I reach out in your direction.
My love,
my perfect partner,
my ebb and flow.
Bonefelt rhythms in faultless synchronicity,
we are flawless in our anticipation of the next steps;
a turn of the head,
a secret smile;
like beautiful markings India-inked on a barn owl
we match
and swirl.
Until I reach once more towards you,
a bit further,
pleading...
and flinch,
start,
stare brokenly,
looking again
and once again.
I pause to watch your face, searching for signs of the
scorching,
the blazing bond we share.
Your calm, familiar gaze,
your deep eyes,
reflect my ardour but you never move in,
never move any closer.
The distance between us is exquisitely matched and timed,
but unreachable

and a coldness swirls into the gap separating us,
chill and lifeless as a satin drapery.
Like a bayonet of ice punched into my heart, I realize you
will not,
can not
deepen.
Will only mimic my echoes
and follow my leading feet...
And I turn,
heartsick and sorrowful,
to begin the search,
once again,
for another;
a partner who will catch fire as I burn,
who will sing the songs only I can hear and
fit our feet into that music,
that endless music,
that only our special twosome can create.
And I close the door sadly,
without a last glance,
leaving the room empty
and the cheap, crooked mirror
hanging dustily alone.

City of Synapses

"There are no rules of architecture for a castle in the clouds." ~ G.K. Chesterton

My thoughts move together,
bow,
clap hands and promenade,
in an unpredictable production.
The setting alternates at whim,
opulent and computerized and groaning with extras
and then,
in the blink of an unseen eye,
there is only a barren stage;
a single, lonely light bulb and a broken milk crate.
Thoughts blossom and burst and run pelting for the exits
and are chased on their swift lizard feet into corners
and gathered into fantastical bouquets of chameleons
that flip through color changes like a short-circuiting mood ring.
I wonder at the traffic encased in my woolly hat as I make
my way down a city sidewalk
and I wonder how many changes of scenery each passerby
carries within them,
their placid faces belying the stormy seas and ship of dreams,
or of fools,
sailing inside.
Our thoughts are like a city of clouds,
skyscrapers of disappearing ink,
a bridge built of sighs;
and we compose,
we fashion,
we grow
these complex structures without ever meeting the architect
face to face,

those blueprints rolled and stored away in the deeply-hidden vaults of the *élan vital*.
This city of synapses and worlds within worlds.
Look closely;
my calm face and eyes give you no hint of the chaos I am master of.
In this secret city,
in this magic I have created, birthed and nurtured from impossible seeds,
I am the lone Adept.
Only here,
in my poetry,
does the scope and grandeur of my hidden world seep through.
Only here can the combined light from a sunrise production, both the grotesque and the heartstoppingly beautiful,
be seen.
Welcome.

In My Very Bones

"In the bleak midwinter, frosty wind made moan,
Earth stood hard as iron, water like a stone;
Snow had fallen, snow on snow, snow on snow,
In the bleak midwinter, long ago." ~ Christina Rossetti

It's in my very bones, this coldness;
the veins of me are chilled,
shivering;
and I sit as close to the candle as I can,
staring at its glowing pulse.
Pinocchio burnt his own feet off longing to be real,
longing to be warm to his own touch.
But who will touch me now?
Is there one who will find me wandering,
guide me to the hearth,
lend me a blanket and allow me to shed the internal icicles
my mind has clothed me in?
Or will I continue this madness dance, this solitary minuet,
alone with the shades?
Once, my spirit took wing suddenly,
soared briefly toward the sun,
but collided like a bird against a window
and fell back stunned, scraped and aching.
I scratch at the forming scars until they bleed, thinking to
reach and release this
thing,
this frigid spectre that stitches me up in garments of
lamentation and near-death frost.
But I remain both here and not here,
a reflection of myself in a pale cool pool.
One who wanders, searching out the light and gazing with
hungry eyes at chimney smoke curling like a beckoning
finger,
now praying that even this small candle could break the spell,

unbind this coldness
and bring me into fire,
if that's what it takes to melt this iron heart,
this coffin of ice.
To crack the very bones and offer up my marrow as a melting comforter,
a coating of wax to keep the drafts from reaching in
and dragging me back.
To sit captive,
shivering, the frost slowly spreading in a graceless pirouette
into my very bones.

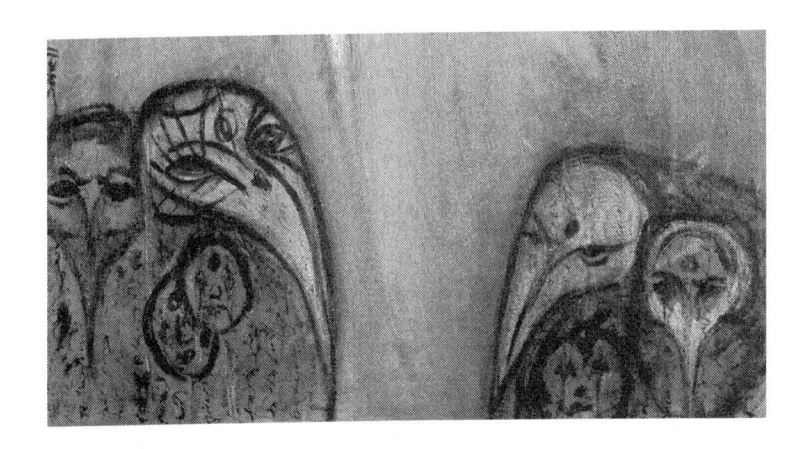

Cherry Wishes

There is a new year on the horizon and wishes clamoring to be born.
Sometimes, special ones hang like cherries on a tree.
The best and biggest,
all round and glossy and winedark with juice,
seem to always
be

    just

        out

            of

                reach.

But these are wishes I would make for you anyway.
There will be bad times along with the good
and dark days with the bright.
I would wish for you the knowledge that all this passes and that light is the one thing the blackness flees,
and my cherry wish would be that you have a friend to remind you of that and to sit warmly next to you
and hold your hand when its dark.
The next wish is that you take pleasure in what you do and that you can love whatever that is without the adulation of others.
There will always be people seeking to knock you down, and I hope and make another cherry wish that you will always have a friend waiting at the bottom with a pillow. And a kleenex.
Being different is sometimes hard, being alone is sometimes easier.
But a cherry friend is the best of both worlds,

quiet and loud ,
pushy and soft like white sand.
A cozy comfort and a bee sting to get you running when you need to move along.
I wish you the sunwarmed fruit of this kind of love,
this friending, and place for it to grow.
And glad times that stain your lips and fingers
with this special messy kind of magic.
This, above all, I wish for you.
My cherry friend.

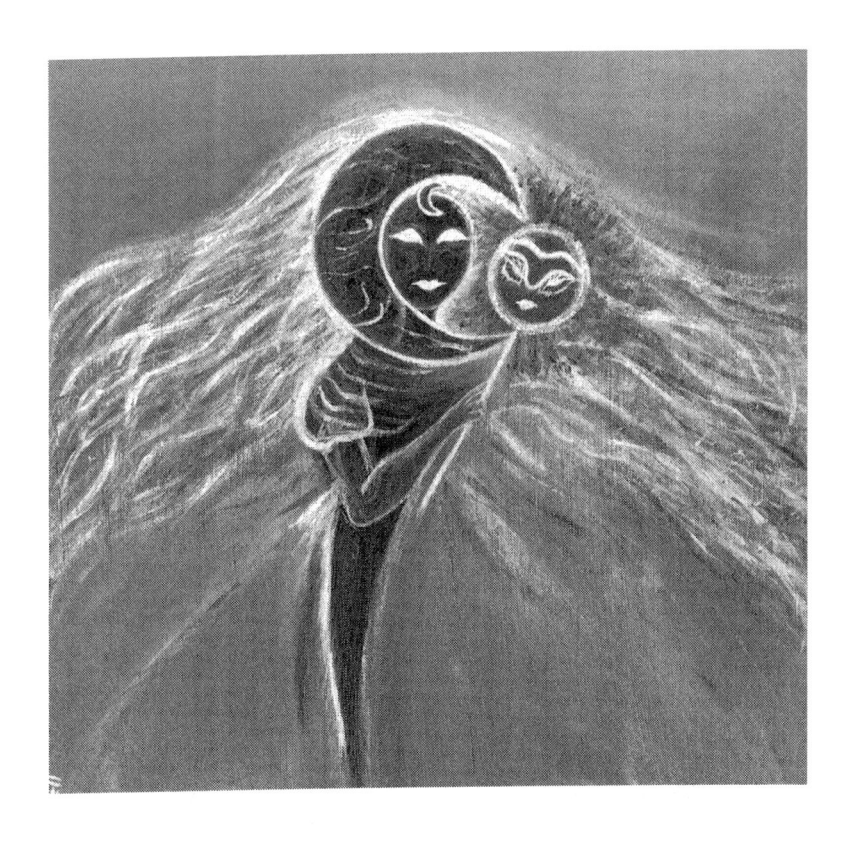

Force of Nature

I am a force of nature, constricted and confined into unnatural situations,
coiled like Jack into a box I was not consulted on,
have not bought nor ordered in my proper size.
Like a wounded bull, provoked once too many times,
the rage has finally taken over
and I'm running headlong into the streets,
marking my track with smeared crimson as I slam against the walls.
Show me kindness and I will follow you,
but I never earned the certificate
for keeping calm when the volcano starts smoking;
and no matter how many flowers you placate it with,
when you reach that point of no return,
she's gonna blow.
And after that river of lava cools,
there will be a kaleidoscope trail of broken bits,
people, relationships, job, hearts, credit,
all tumbling down the side in pebbles.
I mourn their brokenness and hold them up to the light and carry them,
clattering, in my pockets, "just for a while", to look at,
trying to persuade myself it's only a pretty rock.
Trying to persuade myself that, the next time I am in the arena,
I won't let those arrows pierce me;
that I can turn them aside with logic
or politeness.
I just need to learn how.
And God help us,
nature is not a willing teacher.
For she revels in those pressures building and she knows it's imprinted on my cells
to come out of that corner swinging

and scorching everything in my path.
She knows that new growth only comes after a burning.
And that the most magnificent scenes are never of the calm before,
but of the storm.

Poets

To wrap a touch of thought in gauze and carry it carefully to
a warm place where it can rest
and rise;
there is no word to describe the wave that fills your pores and
a scent you have never found but remember so well.
It takes you by the hand,
by the throat sometimes,
and though you try to hold the imprint on your eyes,
you forget so easily
and it falls away into the dusty corners
until swept out and a tingle on the back of your neck makes
you turn
to pick the shining bit up and put it with the others you have
collected and nurtured
to thread onto the poet's crown
and watch it burn with words on fire,
until dropped, sizzling, into the well of souls and cooled with
fresher waters.
This is your honor and your curse,
to glance against but never catch
a thornsharp thirst no wine,
no running stream can alleviate;
never to gaze your fill
and never
reach the end.

Grace, Bitter and Gone

Hello, Gentle Wanderer, Adventurer, Seeker or Bearer of Tales.
There is a backwards mountain
and a river that never flows downhill.
Along a border of silent watchtower trees
you will see in the distance
a hut of rowan wood.
The birds can leave you lost on that ouroboran trail,
or lead you.
You must speak softly and offer them tribut,
grain, berries,
pearls,
long auburn hair,
bits of broken china,
books bound with heartsong,
and if they consent...
you will pass into the valley of the Three.

Three is the number of legend and the circle complete.
There is power in that number,
and magic
and unnamed, untameable force
tapped from a deep well that bursts up like oil
from underground cities of soil and secrets.
The Three know the ways in and out
and the hidden back doors all too well.

Grace bestows the beginnings,
turns the key and gently scrubs the scales from your eyes,
untying a mouth done up in mothspun rough thread
and gifting you with her breath
and a map,
faded to be sure,
but the lines can be seen in certain light

if you know where to look.

Bitter is the refiner,
the keeper of the honing stone
to shape you,
to streamline you,
to make rough edges gentle
or to create sharp points to discourage a lover's hand,
for you can be smoothed or broken by the same stream.

Gone.
Is just...
Gone.
Gone is the least wanted,
but the most faithful, and she waits,
oh so patiently,
amid the bargaining tents,
letting the babble wash over like the tide.
It is always hard to accept that things leaving pain,
like the silverslime from a snail,
are a gift,
but there is blessed relief at the end of an uphill journey in
nothing more than the stopping.

Grace, Bitter and Gone.
Sisters,
mothers,
whores,
destroyers,
saint and sinner wearing the same robes;
and their countenance changes with each grain of the
hourglass.
You have sought and found this place and these Revenants.
Now, how do you answer?
Will you bow or cower?
Can your soul stand the scrutiny?

Will your cheek soften or shrink at the faintest of their kisses,
as if stroked with tree twigs?
And,
most importantly,
what will it be that you carry away with you?

In My Silence

"*Words dazzle and deceive because they are mimed by the face. But black words on a white page are the soul laid bare.*" ~ Guy de Maupassant

To speak aloud the words my heart beats out
would slice my mouth and the
very air escaping would catch fire.
My hands can only fumble with the pen and leave words
cobbled together like scattered pieces of a puzzle.
If someone takes the time to sort and fit them together,
they can read my life
and sit with me in my silence
to watch the storm to blow over,
bend the trees and rainwash the pain away.

Melissa

It's gold I can feel and see first,
gold of honey and wings and delicate wax.
Feel the time and slowness and evenness of it,
walls not content to merely house but curves that hum and
cradle and move you along,
here now,
here now.
My wings,
my stripes,
my head of brass and oil and poppy.
Scents collide and cajole and mingle with the visions in my
head.
Dreams? Memories?
All soft, all fragrant.
Open your mouth and let your tongue weep.
Let it grow heavy on the sweetness.
I rise into the dawn and hold my self as tightly as I can,
as long as I can,
delaying the moment of unfurling so that the pleasure is
tenfold and,
look now, the sun is also gold
and nods to me
in this intimate fellowship,
this airy worship of light we share.

My language is my dance and my sting is not given lightly.
To sting is to die and it must be momentous,
it is to mark the one stung as savior.
And the wax receives my husk,
my shining, emptied capsule,
with love and covering ease
and builds me into the wall of memories.
Gold.
I am gold.

Keys

Her hair was full of stars,
his eyes were full of secrets,
and both of them had keys to hidden doors.
Behind one of them; a stairway to another land
where she was a princess and he was a frog,
but that was alright because they both loved the water.
Behind the other one
nobody knew,
because as soon as anyone living drew near
the deep and ravenous growling began
while the door thudded as if by a large body hurling itself.
How they both came to possess the keys is a story best told
another time,
but there are an infinite number of doors
and a limitless array of unique and surprising
and enterprising
keys.
Most of them unlock and lock,
some only lock,
the maker of Keys gives them only after very careful
consideration
and his eyes are full of secrets also.

Keys 2

There are doors which remain unnoticed by people hurrying
past with their lists and
their phones and music
none of them show up on blueprints
or have nameplates
or doorbells
although sometimes on certain nights
they glow.
There are keys that will unlock them,
but not the usual type.
You don't get them from hardware stores,
they never allow themselves to be lost,
they aren't tagged with souvenirs from an island vacation
or a rabbit's foot,
and the people who keep them
won't tell you who it was that gave (gifted) them
or what they unlock
or much of anything else.
They just smile quietly
and even when you try and focus you
can't
seem
to see
them
anymore
and this amuses them.

Keys 3 : The Door

Climb the steel staircase,
round and dizzying round.
At the top there is a door.
You may have to look with other eyes to see it,
but it's there
trust me.
Take the key, the one you don't like to think about much,
the one the Keymaker gave you
the night you met
and you knew him in an instant
and loved him a breath later,
although you didn't know who
or what
he was
and the key seemed like it had always
(loved) belonged to you.
Use it,
open the door,
walk in,
no –
stride in like you own it,
for in truth you do,
and what you find in that place
behind a door that is not there,
opened with a key that isn't possible,
will be as familiar as your own shadow.

Keys 4 : The Keymaker

Before time,
before doors and locks,
there were keys
and there was the Keymaker,
with the knowledge to call and create
a deep metallic binding,
a friendship
in his kin, his keys
some he fashioned,
others he just delivered;
but every one of them imprinted by his hand.

Death was well pleased when he received the keys
that secured the mighty doors of Hades
and thanked the Keymaker,
offering him a boon, a favor;
but the Keymaker knew better than to accept,
for death may be a gift in its proper place and time,
yet it is never wise to draw his attention.

Scar Tissue

Old words,
old wounds.
Words shot in anger,
in ego,
in fear,
my heart being an endless target,
while my easily-filled eyes tell you when you've scored.
Old words,
old wounds,
rise up like marching furrows.
The scar tissue has made lines
like grimacing smiles,
a map of the ways a person can be split in two,
can be ripped apart,
and still live.
No magician with his chain-bright saw can do so well.

This Is The End

This is the end.
The paved road stops here.
I have searched out the paths and the passwords,
the highways and right ways,
and talked the talk.
All golden tickets sought out and coveted,
yet they all crumbled,
leaving my purse empty and my fingers green with the
falsehoods smearing off of them.
And I am...
tired.
I have expanded myself to be heard,
to be seen,
to be taken seriously,
not for a ride
or at face value
and still the on-the-job training fell too short
and I have been invited to wander once again.

Good bye,
good luck,
good riddance.

I will no longer reach out,
no longer expand.
I will contract instead to feel my experience,
my self
at its purest,
its most powerful.
A star's last breath is its brightest
and instead of begging for a map to the neon-lit crowd-
pleasing intersections,
I will choose my own way,
build my own bridges

and burn
oh so brightly
with them.

Made in the USA
Charleston, SC
23 September 2015